RUBANK EDUCATIONAL LIBRARY No. 141

T0116692

FRENCH HORN

Vol. I

WM. GOWER
AND
H. VOXMAN

**AN OUTLINED COURSE OF STUDY
DESIGNED TO FOLLOW UP ANY
OF THE VARIOUS ELEMENTARY
AND INTERMEDIATE METHODS**

RUBANK ®

HAL•LEONARD ®
CORPORATION
7777 W. BLUEMOUND RD. P.O. BOX 13819 MILWAUKEE, WI 53213

NOTE

THE RUBANK ADVANCED METHOD for French Horn is published in two volumes, the course of study being divided in the following manner:

Vol. I
- Keys of C, F, G, Bb, and D Major.
- Keys of A, D, E, G, and B Minor.

Vol. II
- Keys of Eb, A, Ab, E, Db, and B Major.
- Keys of C, F#, F, and C# Minor.

PREFACE

THIS METHOD is designed to follow any of the various Elementary and Intermediate instruction series, or Elementary instruction series comprising two or more volumes, depending upon the previous development of the student. The authors have found it necessary in their teaching experience to draw from many sources in order to provide a progressive course of study. The present publication assembles in two volumes the material essential to a well-rounded musical development.

THE OUTLINES, one of which is included in each of the respective volumes, tend to afford an objective picture of the student's progress. They will facilitate the ranking of members in a large ensemble or they may serve as a basis for awards of merit. In addition, a one-sided development along strictly technical or strictly melodic lines is avoided. The use of these outlines, however, is not imperative and they may be discarded at the discretion of the teacher.

NOTATION: Music for the French Horn is written in both the treble and bass clefs. In the bass clef two manners of notation are employed, the old and the new:

In this method the new notation is used throughout.

Wm. Gower — H. Voxman

Table of Harmonics for French Horn

The seventh harmonic is too flat and the eleventh harmonic is too sharp to be used satisfactorily.

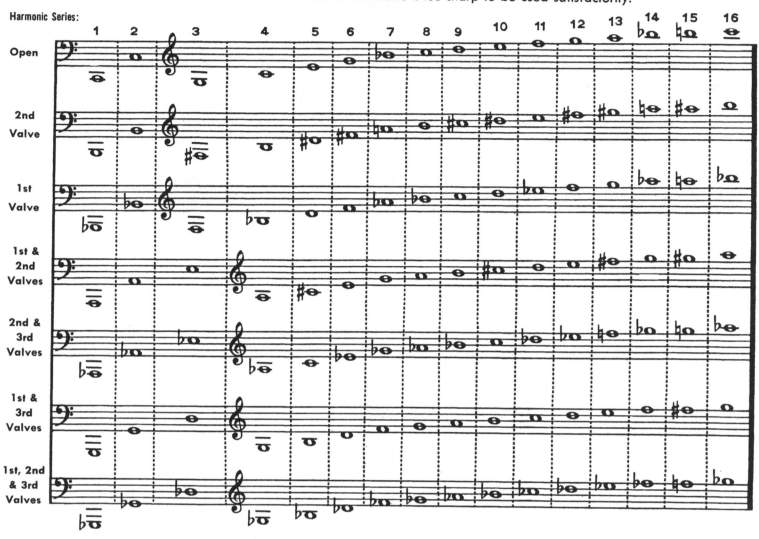

Chromatic Fingering Chart

Regular fingerings are for the F Horn; parenthetical fingerings are for the Bb Horn. The *Third Valve* may be used as an alternate fingering for the *First and Second Valves* on either the F Horn or the Bb Horn.

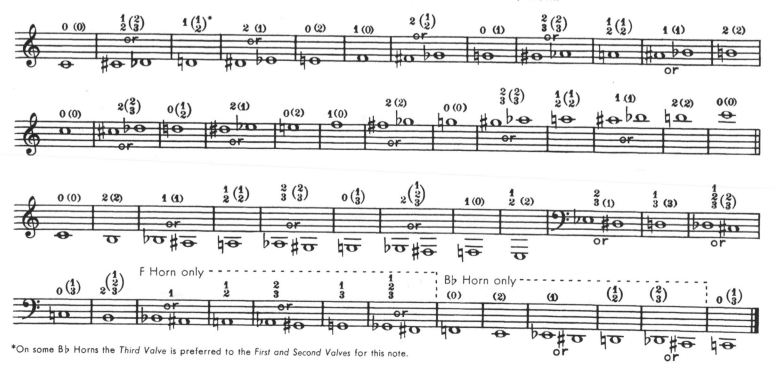

*On some Bb Horns the *Third Valve* is preferred to the *First and Second Valves* for this note.

The Double Horn

The many advantages of the Double Horn have gradually caused it to supercede the Single F Horn and the Single B♭ Horn. The modern Double Horn has an effective over-all length of approximately twelve feet when played in F.   When played in B♭, the length is approximately nine feet. The primary advantage of the B♭ Horn is the greater certainty of striking the correct tone in the upper register.

Performers and teachers differ as to the note in the scale where the changeover from F to B♭ should be made. Without altering the fingering, it is possible to press the thumb valve on any tone between G♯ and C inclusive; e. g., "A" (second space) may be fingered 1st and 2nd valves either with or without the thumb valve. The authors recommend that the change, in most cases, be made at C♯ thereby insuring the most uniform tone quality.

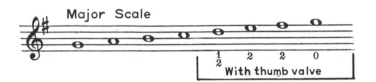

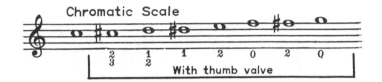

For acoustical reasons certain tones of the lower register are produced more easily on the B♭ Horn.

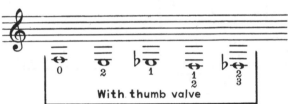

Transposition

A thorough knowledge of transposition is indispensable to the serious student of the French Horn. Although most recent publications provide parts for the Horn in F, the student will frequently be obliged to execute Horn parts in E♭ (in the band) and in high B♭, A, A♭, G, F♯, F, E, E♭, D, D♭, C, B and low B♭ (in the orchestra).

Transposition can be accomplished with either the aid of the clefs or according to the intervals. In this country the most frequently used method is that of the intervals. Thus, E♭ Horn parts are played one whole step (a major second) lower than they are written:

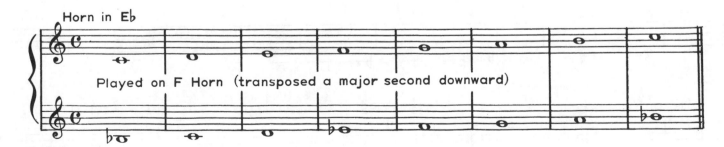

AMERICA

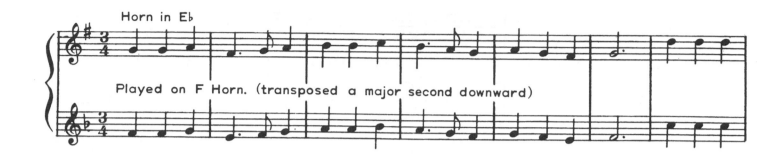

Muting

Muting is done by placing the right hand inside the bell of the **French Horn** so as to all but close the bell. The hand is inserted far enough to raise the pitch exactly one half-step. This raising of the pitch obliges the player to transpose the muted note one half-step lower.

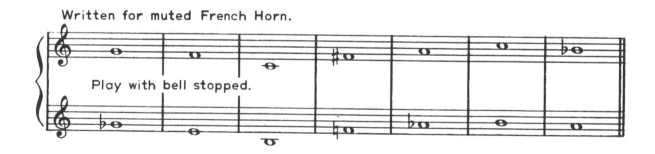

Various words and signs are used to indicate the use of the muted or stopped horn. The German terms *gestopft* or *gedümpft*, the French *bouché*, the Italian *con sordino*, all mean to mute the horn. In addition to these terms the symbol + is frequently used. To indicate the open horn after a muted passage, the words *open* or *natural*, *öffen* (German), *ouvert* (French), and *senza sordino* (Italian), are used. The symbol o is also common.

Some players prefer to use brass mutes instead of the hand. These mutes are of two types, a transposing and a non-transposing variety.

Transposition Studies

PRACTICE AND GRADE REPORT

SECOND SEMESTER

Student's Name _____

Date _____

Week	Sun.	Mon.	Tue.	Wed.	Thu.	Fri.	Sat.	Total	Parent's Signature	Grade
1										
2										
3										
4										
5										
6										
7										
8										
9										
10										
11										
12										
13										
14										
15										
16										
17										
18										
19										
20										

Semester Grade

Instructor's Signature _____

FIRST SEMESTER

Student's Name _____

Date _____

Week	Sun.	Mon.	Tue.	Wed.	Thu.	Fri.	Sat.	Total	Parent's Signature	Grade
1										
2										
3										
4										
5										
6										
7										
8										
9										
10										
11										
12										
13										
14										
15										
16										
17										
18										
19										
20										

Semester Grade

Instructor's Signature _____

OUTLINE
OF
RUBANK ADVANCED METHOD
FOR
FRENCH HORN, Vol. I
BY
Wm. Gower and H. Voxman

UNIT	SCALES and ARPEGGIOS	(Key)	MELODIC INTERPRE-TATION	ARTICU-LATION	FLEXIBILITY EXERCISES	ORNA-MENTS	SOLOS	UNIT COM-PLETED
1	10 (1) 11 (5)	C	22 (1)	47 (1)	61 (1)	64 (1)	69 (1)	
2	10 (2) 11 (6)	C	22 (2)	47 (2)	61 (1)	64 (1)	69 (1)	
3	10 (3) 11 (7)	C	23 (3)	47 (3)	61 (1)	64 (2)	69 (1)	
4	11 (4) 11 (8)	C	23 (4)	48 (4)	61 (2)	64 (2)	69 (1)	
5	11 (9)	a	24 (5)	48 (5)	61 (2)	64 (3)	69 (1)	
6	12 (10) 12 (12)	a	24 (6)	48 (6)	61 (2)	64 (3)	69 (1)	
7	12 (11)	a	25 (7)	49 (7)	61 (3)	64 (4)	69 (2)	
8	12 (13) (14) (15)	a	26 (8)	49 (8)	61 (3)	64 (5)	69 (2)	
9	13 (16) 14 (20)	F	26 (9)	49 (9)	61 (3)	65 (6)	69 (2)	
10	13 (17) 14 (21)	F	27 (10)	50 (10)	61 (4)	65 (7)	69 (2)	
11	13 (18) 14 (22)	F	27 (10)	50 (11)	61 (4)	65 (7)	69 (2)	
12	13 (19)	F	28 (11)	50 (12)	61 (4)	65 (8)	69 (2)	
13	14 (23) (25)	d	29 (12)	51 (13)	61 (5)	65 (9)	70 (3)	
14	14 (24)	d	29 (12)	51 (14)	61 (5)	65 (9)	70 (3)	
15	14 (26) 15 (27) (28)	d	30 (13)	52 (15)	61 (5)	65 (9)	70 (3)	
16	15 (29) 16 (33)	G	31 (14)	52 (16)	62 (6)	66 (10)	70 (3)	
17	15 (30) 16 (34)	G	31 (15)	52 (17)	62 (6)	66 (10)	70 (3)	
18	15 (31) 16 (35)	G	32 (16)	53 (18)	62 (6)	66 (11)	70 (3)	
19	15 (32) 16 (36)	G	33 (17)	53 (19)	62 (7)	66 (12)	70 (4)	
20	16 (37)	e	34 (18)	54 (20)	62 (7)	66 (13)	70 (4)	
21	16 (38)	e	35 (19)	54 (21)	62 (7)	66 (13)	70 (4)	
22	17 (39) (40) (41)	e	35 (19)	54 (22)	62 (8)	67 (14)	70 (4)	
23	17 (42) 18 (46)	Bb	36 (20)	55 (23)	62 (8)	67 (15)	70 (4)	
24	17 (43) 18 (47)	Bb	36 (21)	55 (24)	62 (8)	67 (15)	70 (4)	
25	17 (44) 18 (48)	Bb	37 (22)	56 (25)	62 (9)	67 (16)	71 (5)	
26	18 (45)	Bb	38 (23)	56 (26)	62 (9)	67 (17)	71 (5)	
27	18 (49) 19 (53)	g	39 (24)	56 (27)	62 (9)	67 (17)	71 (5)	
28	18 (50) 19 (52) (54)	g	39 (25)	57 (28)	62 (10)	67 (18)	71 (5)	
29	18 (51)	g	39 (25)	57 (29)	62 (10)	68 (19)	71 (5)	
30	19 (55) 20 (59)	D	41 (26)	58 (30)	62 (10)	68 (20)	71 (5)	
31	20 (56) 21 (60)	D	41 (27)	58 (31)	62 (11)	68 (20)	72 (6)	
32	20 (57) 21 (61)	D	42 (28)	58 (32)	62 (11)	68 (21)	72 (6)	
33	20 (58) 21 (62)	D	43 (29)	59 (33)	62 (11)	68 (21)	72 (6)	
34	21 (63)	b	44 (30)	59 (34)	63 (12)	68 (22)	72 (6)	
35	21 (64)	b	45 (31)	60 (35)	63 (12)	68 (22)	72 (6)	
36	21 (65) (66) (67)	b	45 (32)	60 (36)	63 (12)	68 (23)	72 (6)	

NUMERALS designate page number.
ENCIRCLED NUMERALS designate exercise number.
COMPLETED EXERCISES may be indicated by crossing out the rings, thus, .

Scales and Arpeggios

C Major

Copyright MCMXLVII by Rubank, Inc.

Various articulations may be used in the chromatic, the interval and the chord studies at the instructors option.

Exercise in Thirds

Common Chord

Dominant 7th

A Minor

The sign ⌣ indicates a half-step

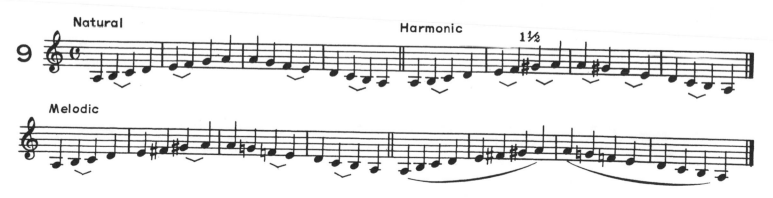

Common Chord

27

Diminished 7th

28

G Major

29

simile

30

simile

31

simile

simile

32

simile

simile

Studies in Melodic Interpretation

For One or Two Part Playing

The following studies are designed to aid in the development of the student's interpretative ability. Careful attention to the marks of expression is essential to effective use of the material. Pencil the technically difficult passages and devote extra time to their mastery.

In rhythmic music in the more rapid tempi (marches, dances, etc.) tones that are equal divisions of the beat are played somewhat detached (staccato). Tones that are equal a beat or are multiples of a beat are held full value. Tones followed by rests are usually held full value. This point should be especially observed in slow music. *These studies may be played a whole tone lower for practice in transposition of Eb Horn music.*

BORTNIANSKY

KÜFFNER

CARNAUD

SCHANTL

Andantino

BERR

7

11

De GOUY

Tempo di bolero

12

Andante affettuoso

14

Marcia

BERR

15

Moderato

Hunters' Chorus

WEBER

Allegretto grazioso

GATTI

17

Andante appassionato

18

Quite slowly

FRANZ

22

Adagio

FORESTIER

24

Vivace

BONNISSEAU

25

Die Lorelei

SILCHER

26

FRANZ

27

Slowly

FORESTIER

Allegro assai

29

Andante sostenuto

De GOUY

30

Studies in Articulation

In all exercises where no tempo is indicated the student should play the study as rapidly as is consistent with tonal control and technical accuracy. The first practice in each exercise should be done very slowly in order that the articulation may be carefully observed.

In allegro tempi, figures similar to 🎵 should be performed 🎵 , etc. The figure 🎵 should be played 🎵 .

The material for these exercises has been taken from the methods of Kling, Franz, Schollar, etc. The studies may be transposed at the option of the teacher.

Andante maestoso

58

60

Flexibility Exercises

Keep the tone well sustained throughout the slur indicated, leaving no gaps between tones. The slur must be made smoothly and evenly by the flexibility of the embouchure. Adhere strictly to the fingerings given.

Lip Trills

Use only the fingerings indicated.

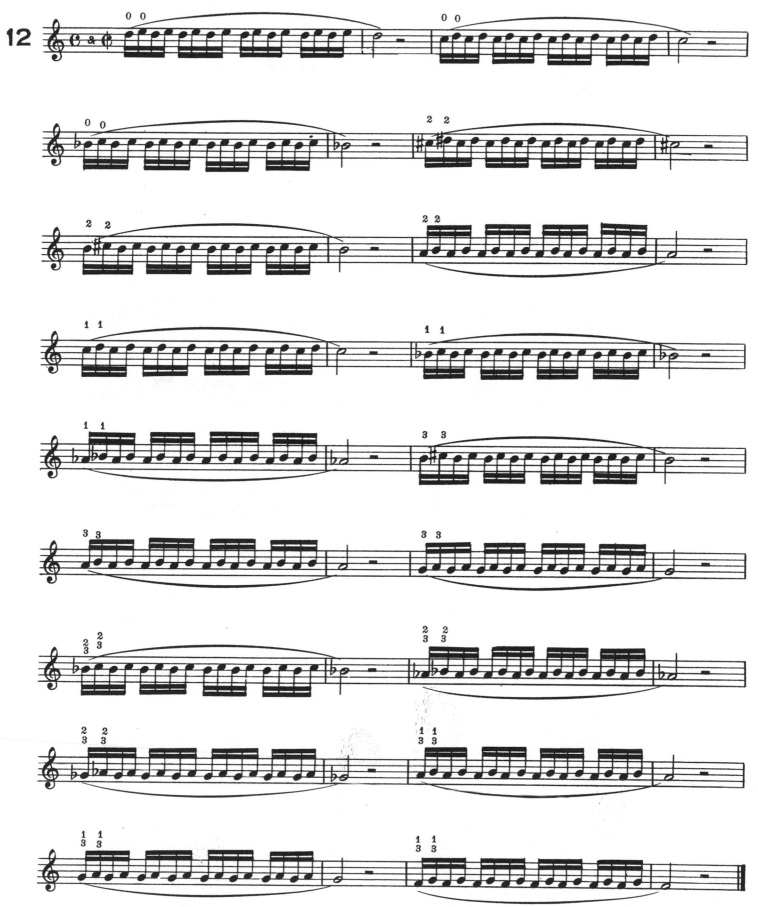

Musical Ornamentation (Embellishments)

The following treatment of ornamentation is by no means complete. It is presented here only as a guide to the execution of those ornaments which the student may encounter at this stage of his musical development. There are different manners of performing the same ornament.

The Trill (Shake)

The trill (or shake) consists of the rapid alternation of two tones. They are represented by the printed note (called the principal note) and the next tone above in the diatonic scale. The interval between the two tones may be either a half-step or a whole-step. The signs for the trill are 𝆖 and 〰.

An accidental when used in conjunction with the trill sign affects the upper note of the trill.

Grace Notes (Appoggiatura)

The grace notes are indicated by notes of a smaller size. They may be divided into two classes: long and short.

Long grace notes

from "Serenade" Haydn

Andante cantabile

In instrumental music of recent composition the short grace notes should occupy as little time as possible and that value is taken preceding the principal note. They may be single, double, triple or quadruple, as the case may be. The single short grace note is printed as a small eighth note with a stroke through its hook. It is not to be accented. Use trill fingerings when fundamental fingerings are too difficult.

Short grace notes

Allegretto

ARBAN

The Mordent

The short mordent (𝄽) consists of a single rapid alternation of the principal note with its lower auxiliary. Two or more alternations are executed in the long mordent.

The inverted mordent (𝄾) does not have the cross line. In it the lower auxiliary is replaced by the upper. It is the more commonly used mordent in music for the wind instruments.

The mordent takes its value from the principal note.

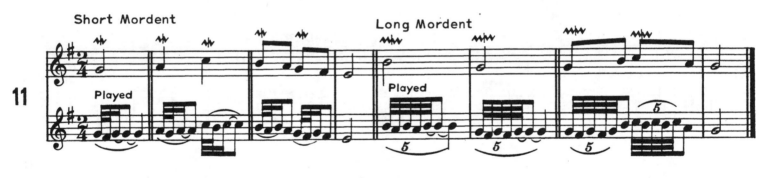

In trills of sufficient length a special ending is generally used whether indicated or not

The closing of the trill consists of two tones: the scale tone below the principal note and the principal note.

In long trills of a solo character, it is good taste to commence slowly and gradually increase the speed. Practice the following exercises in the manner of both examples 1 and 2.

The Turn (Gruppetto)

The turn consists of four tones: the next scale tone above the principal tone, the principle tone itself, the tone below the principal tone, and the principal tone again.

When the ∽ is placed to the right of the note, the principal tone is held almost to its full value, then the turn is played just before the next melody tone. In this case (Ex. 1, 2, 3, 4 and 5) the four tones are of equal length.

When the turn is placed between a dotted note and another note having the same value as the dot (Ex. 6 and 8), the turn is then played with the last note of the turn taking the place of the dot, making two notes of the same value. The turn sign after a dotted note will indicate that one melody note lies hidden in the dot.

Sometimes an accidental sign occurs with the turn, and in this case, when written above the sign, it refers to the highest tone of the turn, but when written below, to the lowest. (Ex. 2 and 1).

When the turn is placed over a note (Ex.3) the tones are usually played quickly, and the fourth tone is then held until the time value of the note has expired.

In the inverted turn (Ex.4) the order of tones is reversed, the lowest one coming first, the principal next, the highest third and the principal tone again, last. The inverted turn is indicated by the ordinary turn sign reversed: ∾ or by ⸮.

The Sandman

Arr. by BRAHMS

Andante

Sailor's Song

GRIEG

Allegro e marcato

By the Sea

SCHUBERT

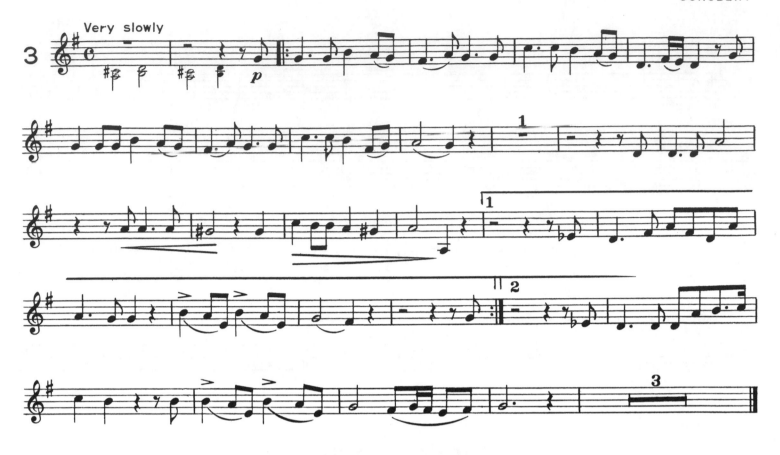

Possenti Numi

MOZART

On Wings of Song

MENDELSSOHN

Romanze
Concerto No.3
(K. 447)

French Horn in F

W. A. MOZART
Edited by H. Voxman